Poetry for Students, Volume 25

Project Editor: Ira Mark Milne

Editorial: Anne Marie Hacht

Rights Acquisition and Management: Edna Hedblad, Lisa Kincade, Timothy Sisler **Manufacturing**: Drew Kalasky

Image Research & Acquisition: Dean Dauphinais, Kelly Quin **Imaging and Multimedia**: Lezlie Light, Mike Logusz **Product Design**: Pamela A. E. Galbreath **Vendor Administration**: Civie Green

Product Manager: Meggin Condino

For more information, contact
Gale, an imprint of Cengage Learning
27500 Drake Rd.
Farmington Hills, MI 48331-3535

individual does not imply endorsement of the editors or publisher. Errors brought to the attention of the publisher and verified to the satisfaction of the publisher will be corrected in future editions.

ISBN-13: 978-0-7876-8715-1
ISBN-10: 0-7876-8715-4
ISSN 1094-7019

Printed in the United States of America
10 9 8 7 6 5 4 3 2 1

Supernatural Love

Gjertrud Schnackenberg 1985

Introduction

In the 1980s, a number of young American poets, Gjertrud Schnackenberg among them, began writing poetry in rhyme and meter rather than in the free verse that had dominated the American poetry scene since the late 1950s. Schnackenberg's "Supernatural Love" is written in iambic pentameter, a meter of five two-syllable feet with the first syllable accented and the second unaccented; it is divided into tercets, or triplets—three-line stanzas in which the last word of each line rhymes with the other two. Thematically, the poem explores the relationship between the history and definitions of certain words and Christian theological doctrine, weaving these elements into a touching anecdote about the relationship between a four-year-old girl and her father.

"Supernatural Love," was first published in Schnackenberg's second collection of poetry, *The Lamplit Answer*, in 1985. It subsequently has been reprinted in many poetry anthologies, including the second edition of the *Norton Anthology of Modern Poetry* (1996). *The Lamplit Answer* was so well received by critics that during the 1980s Schnackenberg was considered one of the outstanding young poets writing in America. Her later publications have solidified her reputation. Much of her work is difficult, but "Supernatural Love" is one of her most accessible poems.

Author Biography

Gjertrud Schnackenberg was born on August 27, 1953, in Tacoma, Washington. Her Lutheran family was of Norwegian descent. Her father, Walter Charles Schnackenberg, taught at Pacific Lutheran University in Tacoma, a college that was founded by Norwegian immigrants. As Schnackenberg grew up, she enjoyed a very close relationship with her father, and his early death in 1973 affected her profoundly. At the time, she was an undergraduate student at Mount Holyoke College, from which she graduated summa cum laude with a bachelor of arts degree in 1975. At Mount Holyoke, students and professors alike were aware of her remarkable talent, and in 1973 and 1974 she won the prestigious Glascock Prize for poetry. This recognition brought her work to the attention of influential poets. Her first published collection, *Portraits and Elegies* (1982), was enthusiastically received by critics and established her as one of the foremost young poets in America. Many of the poems in the collection were tributes to her late father, recalling the times she had spent with him. In "Nightfishing," for example, she remembers a predawn fishing trip they made together; in "Returning North," she describes a trip to Norway they took when she was ten years old.

During the 1980s, Schnackenberg won many awards, including the Lavan Younger Poets Award from the Academy of American Poets (1983), the

Rome Prize in Literature (1983–1984) from the American Academy and Institute of Arts and Letters, and an Amy Lowell Traveling Prize (1984–1985), which enabled her to spend two years in Italy. She was also awarded an honorary doctorate from Mount Holyoke College in 1985, the same year in which her second collection, *The Lamplit Answer*, was published. This collection contains the poem "Supernatural Love."

Schnackenberg has published her poetry infrequently. It was seven years before her third collection, *A Gilded Lapse of Time*, appeared in 1992. *The Throne of Labdacus*, poems based on the Oedipus legend, followed in 2000. In the same year, *Supernatural Love: Poems 1976–1992* was published, containing selections from her previously published work.

Schnackenberg's first marriage, to Paul Smyth, ended in divorce. She married Robert Nozick, a Harvard philosophy professor, in 1987. They had met after Nozick read *The Lamplit Answer* in the Harvard bookstore in 1985 and decided that he wanted to meet the author. They shared a life of art, philosophy, writing, and travel until Nozick's death from cancer in 2002.

Poem Summary

Stanzas 1-4

In "Supernatural Love," the speaker tells of an incident that involved herself and her father when she was four years old. The poem is set in a dimly lit study in which father and daughter are present. The father is at a dictionary stand, consulting a dictionary, which is illumined by a lamp. He holds a magnifying glass in his hand and scans the dictionary, running his finger down the page in order to find the word he is looking for. Then he holds the magnifying glass still above the definition of the word *carnation*. He bends closer to the dictionary and puts his finger on the page and reads the definition. The definition of one word seems to help him make some kind of as yet unspecified connection with something much larger.

Stanzas 5-8

The child, who is doing cross-stitch on a needlework sampler, imitates her father by bringing her sewing needle to her eye, which allows her to see her father through the eye of the needle "as through a lens ground for a butterfly" (stanza 4). It is likely that she is sitting very near him, to be close to the light; as she looks up at him, she sees his eyes "magnified and blurred" (stanza 3) through the lens of his magnifying glass. The poet then compares the girl looking through the needle's eye to a butterfly probing a flower ("flower-hallways") with its long, tubelike mouth in order to suck up the nectar it needs. Perhaps the nectar is located in the "room / shadowed and fathomed" within the flower, to which the "hallways" lead. These rooms are imagined by the poet to be as dark as the dimly lit study in which the girl sits. Another simile follows, in which the father, poring over a dictionary and reading the Latin derivation of the word he is looking up ("Latin blossom"), is compared to a scholar bending over a tomb to read the inscription on it.

The four-year-old girl then spills her pins and needles on the floor as she tries "to stitch the word 'Beloved'" (stanza 8) in her sampler, cross-stitch by cross-stitch. Although she cannot read, she feels connected by her needle to the word. She refers to her needle as dangerous for reasons that will become apparent later in the poem.

Stanzas 9-13

The girl's father is looking up the word *carnation* in the dictionary to find out why his daughter calls carnations "Christ's flowers." He knows that she can give no explanation for this other than to say "Because." All she knows (the adult speaker's voice explains) is that for some reason, the root meanings of words convey a silent, preverbal message to her, just as the threads at the back of her sampler (themselves like roots) contribute in an unseen way to the word "beloved" she is trying to create, which has as its root the word *love*.

Her father then reads out the definition of *carnation* in the dictionary. It is a pink variety of clove, from the Latin root *carnatio*, meaning flesh. The adult speaker's voice suggests that it is as if the essential oils of the flower are sending the fragrance of Christ through the room. When the girl hears this definition, the odor of carnations floats up to her, and she imagines the stems of the flowers squeaking in her scissors as they are cut. With that cut, the stems seem to speak, or at least a voice is heard, saying, *"Child, it's me"* (stanza 13).

Stanzas 14-16

Her father then turns the pages of the dictionary to the word *clove* and reads the definition aloud to her. The clove is a spice dried from a flower bud. He reads further that the word is from the French word, *clou*, meaning "a nail." Twice he rereads the information, as if he has not understood it the first time. Then he gazes, standing completely still, contemplating. He again mulls over the fact that clove, *clou*, means "a nail."

The girl continues stitching "beloved." Then the girl's needle catches within the threads. An italicized phrase follows, *"Thy blood so dearly bought"* (stanza 16), which is a reference to the doctrine that Christ's blood bought salvation for all. The relevance of this becomes apparent in the first line of the next stanza.

Stanzas 17-19

As she tries to free the needle from the thread in which it has been caught up, the girl accidentally pricks her finger with the needle. It cuts to the bone. She lifts her hand and sees that she has actually driven the needle through her own flesh ("it is myself I've sewn"). Now the threads she sees are threads of her own blood as it trickles down her hand. Startled and in pain, she lifts her hand and calls out for her father, "Daddy daddy."

Her father touches her injured finger lightly, as "lightly as he touched the page" (stanza 19) of the dictionary just a few moments earlier. The poem ends with a reiteration of the significance of the definitions of the words he looked up: the French and Latin roots of the words *carnation* and *clove* explain why the four-year-old child was correct in her association of carnations with Christ.

Themes

Poetic Symbolism and Theological Doctrine

The theme of supernatural love, the love of God for humans, is emphasized by the activity of both father and daughter. The father investigates the root meanings of words and discovers why the carnation is a perfect symbol for the incarnation and crucifixion of Christ, since *carnation* comes from the Latin root meaning "flesh" and a carnation is a type of clove, which comes from the French word *clou*, meaning "nail." Thus a kind of poetic shorthand symbolizing a central Christian doctrine is set up, in which flesh equals incarnation and nail equals crucifixion. In Christian theology, Jesus Christ is the son of God, sent by God to save humankind from sin. By dying on the Cross, Christ redeemed humans from the curse of the Original Sin committed by Adam and Eve in the Garden of Eden. Christ was wholly divine but was born into human flesh and was therefore fully human too.

The activity of the four-year-old girl as she stitches "Beloved" in her needlework sampler suggests the inner meaning of the incarnation, death, and resurrection of Christ. "Beloved" is a reference to Christ, especially to the passage in the Gospels that follows Christ's baptism. A voice from heaven is heard saying, "This is my beloved Son, with whom I am well pleased" (Matthew 3:17). The incarnation of Christ is a demonstration of God's love for the world, since he sent his only son, whom he loved, to redeem it. The girl's cross-stitches in her sampler, indicated in the poem by the letter *X* (stanza 8), graphically suggest the cross on which Christ was crucified. Thus, just as her father, in his investigation in the dictionary, unearths a link between incarnation and crucifixion, so does the girl, in her needlework, stumble upon a link between supernatural love (the significance of the word *beloved* when applied to Christ) and the crucifixion.

Finally, the poem brings father and daughter together in a small but symbolic interaction that not only establishes their close relationship but also echoes the relationship between God and his son Christ in Christian theology. When the girl pricks herself with the needle and bleeds, she re-creates within herself in miniature the drama of the crucifixion, when the nails pierced Christ's flesh. Her call, "Daddy daddy—" (stanza 18) is an echo of the cry of Jesus to his father on the cross: "My God, my God, why hast thou forsaken me?" (Matthew 27:46). Resurrection and salvation are implied at the end of the poem when the girl's father, now also identified with the heavenly father, touches her lightly to heal her. In a theological context, this suggests the absolute human dependence on God for salvation.

The theological framework of the poem is reinforced by clusters of images. After the girl pricks her finger with the needle, she says, "the threads of blood my own" (stanza 17), which suggests the relevance of the crucifixion to her own experience and also links her stitching of the word *beloved* to the crucifixion, since the threads she is using are now stained with her blood and the blood associated with Christ's saving death has just been mentioned, in stanza 16 (*"Thy blood so dearly bought"*). Further, the blood-thread image is linked to the incarnation of Christ, in the words "my threads like stems" (stanza 16), meaning the stems of carnations. In this way, the images all weave together to create a tapestry of meaning that reinforces the theme of supernatural love manifesting through the incarnation and crucifixion of Christ. The child speaker, who intuits much more than she understands intellectually, is used by the poet to create and communicate poetic symbolism through the interplay between the root meanings of the words the child's father looks up and theological concepts.

Topics for Further Study

- Write an essay in which you compare and contrast "Supernatural Love" with Sylvia Plath's poem "Daddy," from her collection *Ariel*, or Andrew Hudgins's poem "Elegy for My Father, Who Is Not Dead," in Hudgins's collection *The Never-Ending* (1991). What does each poem reveal about the relationship between son or daughter and father?
- Write a short poem on any topic in metered verse that rhymes. Try to introduce variations in the meter, so that the poem does not sound monotonous. Then take the same theme and write the poem in free verse. Write a separate brief essay in which you state which is the better poem and why and which was easier to write.
- Make a class presentation in which you discuss the question of whether poetry has any relevance for modern life. What do poetry and other forms of literature add to life that cannot be gained from business, science, or technology? Why are the arts needed at all?
- Consider whether popular song

lyrics, for example, rap or country-and-western songs, can be thought of as poetry. What poetic techniques do these songs use and why? Are some advertising jingles poetry? What poetic techniques do they use and why? Make a class presentation, using examples from CDs or music videos to illustrate your points.

Style

Variations in Rhyme

The poem is written in tercets, which are stanzas of three lines that contain a single rhyme. In other words, the endings of all three lines rhyme. In stanza 1, for example, "dictionary-stand," "understand," and "hand" all rhyme; in stanza 2, "lens," "suspends," and "bends" all rhyme; and so on. In some stanzas, the rhymes are approximate rather than exact, and these are known as off rhymes, near rhymes, or imperfect rhymes. Stanza 10, ending with "because," "messages," and "does," is an example in which the vowel sounds are different in each word.

Stanza 11 contains an example of what is called eye rhyme, in which the endings of words are spelled the same and thus look as if they rhyme, but they are pronounced differently. These words are "move," "love," and "clove." In stanza 15, all three lines end in the word "nail," an example of what is called identical rhyme or tautological rhyme. When a rhymed word at the end of a line falls on a stressed syllable, it is known as a masculine rhyme. Examples of masculine rhymes occur in stanza 3 with "blurred," "word," and "heard"; in stanza 4 with "string," "thing," and "bring"; in stanza 6 with "room," "gloom," and "tomb"; and in stanza 7 with "pore," "four," and "floor." When a rhymed word at the end of the line falls on an unstressed syllable, it is known as a feminine rhyme. An example occurs in stanza 18 with "agony, "daddy," and "injury."

Variations in Meter

The overall meter of the poem is iambic pentameter. Meter is the rhythm of stressed and unstressed syllables in a poetic foot. A foot consists of a combination of stressed and unstressed syllables (sometimes called strong stresses and weak, or light, stresses). An iambic foot (or, in its noun form, an iamb) is an unstressed syllable followed by a stressed syllable. Iambic pentameter is made up of five iambic feet to a line. One of the clearest examples of iambic pentameter in the poem is in stanza 14: "He turns the page to 'Clove' and reads aloud." Another line in which the iambic meter is especially clear is in stanza 10: "The way the thread behind my sampler does."

Poets make subtle alterations to the meter of their poems. These alterations keep the poems from becoming monotonous and sing-song. Often the alterations are used to bring sharper attention to a word or concept. A common variation in iambic pentameter is to invert the first foot in a line. In "Supernatural Love," stanza 1 begins not with an iamb but with a trochee, "Touches," in which a stressed syllable is followed by an unstressed one. Other examples of an inverted first iambic foot (or a trochaic foot, to use the adjective form of *trochee*), in which the variation stands out against the basic metrical rhythm, occur in stanza 6 ("Shadowed"), stanza 8 ("trying"), and stanza 12 ("Christ's fra-"). In stanza 10, there is another kind of variation in the first foot, a spondee, "Wordroot," in which both syllables are stressed. This spondaic foot (the adjective form of *spondee*) is then followed by another metrical variation, a trochee ("blossom") rather than an iamb.

Caesura

A caesura is a pause within the line, often indicated by a comma or a period. Poets will use caesura to create emphasis and variety in a line of verse. In stanza 7, there is a caesura: "Over the Latin blossom. I am four." Stanza 15 contains two caesuras, the second longer than the first: "He gazes, motionless. 'Meaning a nail.'" The caesuras, which slow the poem down, express the sense of stillness conveyed by the meaning of the words. The caesuras in the last lines of stanza 2 ("Above the word 'Carnation.' Then he bends") and stanza 4 ("That's smaller than the 'universe.' I bring") help illustrate another technique the poet uses. The placing of the period near the end of the line ensures that the sentence that follows it carries over to the next stanza. This is known as a run-on line, in which the end of the line does not correspond with a completed unit of meaning. Schnackenberg makes frequent use of run-on lines in this poem, especially in the last lines of the stanzas.

Historical Context

The New Formalism

In the 1960s and 1970s, most poets in America wrote in free verse, which paid no attention to rhyme or meter or traditional poetic form. The predominant form was the personal lyric. During the 1980s, this started to change, and a movement emerged known as the New Formalism, in which poets returned to writing verse in traditional forms. The trend is noted by the poet and critic Dana Gioia in his 1987 essay "Notes on the New Formalism." He points out that two of the most impressive first poetry volumes of the decade are Brad Leithauser's *Hundreds of Fireflies* (1983) and Vikram Seth's *The Golden Gate* (1986), both of which were written entirely in formal verse. He might well have added Schnackenberg's *Portraits and Elegies* (1982) and *The Lamplit Answer* (1985), since she, too, was a poet working exclusively with traditional poetic forms. Gioia's own first collection of poetry, *Daily Horoscope* (1986), is also a contribution to the new movement.

Gioia notes that the new development is quite radical because, in 1980, most young poets had been trained so exclusively on free verse that they were unable to write poems in traditional meters. The literary culture in which they were raised emphasized the visual (sight) rather than the aural (sound), and poems were seen as words on a page rather than something to be read out loud. "Literary journalism has long declared it [traditional form] defunct, and most current anthologies present no work in traditional forms by Americans written after 1960," writes Gioia. He argues that the New Formalism, which was a revival not only of rhyme and meter but also of narrative poetry (that is, poetry that tells a story) came about as a reaction to the fact that poetry had lost its broad popular audience. It had become overly intellectualized, and poets were mostly confined to the academy, where they wrote poems that were read only by a small coterie of other poets, graduate students in creative writing, editors of poetry magazines and small presses, and grant-giving organizations. New Formalists, on the other hand, saw themselves as populists, which means in this context that they wrote for people who were not necessarily highly educated. Many of the New Formalists also worked outside the university setting. Gioia, for example, made his living as a businessman. Other poets associated with New Formalism in the 1980s included Marilyn Hacker, William Logan, Timothy Steele, Robert McDowell, Mark Jarman, and Mary Jo Salter.

Compare & Contrast

- **1980s:** The emergence of New Formalism in American poetry challenges the dominance of free verse.

Today: The coexistence of free verse and formalism in contemporary poetry creates a highly diverse literary culture.

- **1980s:** The poetry slam is invented in a jazz club in Chicago in 1986. It treats poetry as a competition, with cash prizes for the winner. Poetry slams spread to other major cities in the United States and attract large audiences, showing that poetry can still be popular.

  Today: Poetry slams continue to flourish nationwide. The National Slam attracts teams from all over the United States, Canada, and other countries. Academic credentials are unimportant for success in poetry slams. Performers must be able to project their poetry to an audience, and showmanship counts as much as poetic skill. The vocal delivery of successful poetry slam performers is similar to hip-hop music.

- **1980s:** In a decade of political and cultural conservatism, momentum builds for large budget cuts in federal subsidies for the arts, including the National Endowment for the Arts (NEA) and the National Endowment for the Humanities

(NEH). This is, in part, because several controversial artists supported by NEA grants produce work that offends mainstream religious sensibilities.
Today: After the 1990s, in which some Republican congressmen called for the abolition of the NEA and the NEA budget was cut by 40 percent, the NEA and NEH receive relatively favorable treatment from the administration of George W. Bush. At a time of budget cuts, both endowments remain stable in the allocation of federal funds. In 2005, for financial year 2006, Congress approves an increase of $4.4 million for the NEA.

The New Formalism was greeted with some hostility by poets and critics who preferred free verse to traditional forms. The term *New Formalism* itself was coined by hostile critics, who believed that traditional poetic forms were artificial and elitist and stifled free expression. In his essay "What's New about the New Formalism," Robert McPhillips describes the attack on the new movement by critics who "labeled these new formal poems as the products of 'yuppie' poets for whom a poem is mere artifice, something to be valued as a material object; or, more perniciously, as the product of a neo-conservative *Zeitgeist." (Zeitgeist* is a German word that can be translated as "spirit of the times.") The argument is that there was nothing new about New Formalism, that it was merely a throwback to what was regarded as the dry, academic poetry of the 1950s, against which free verse was a welcome revolution. McPhillips argues that this is untrue. He believes that the New Formalists' "attention to form has allowed a significant number of younger poets to think and communicate clearly about their sense of what is of most human value—love, beauty, mortality."

Sometimes the New Formalism has been referred to as the Expansive Movement, meaning that poetry was being expanded in terms of the number of forms that were considered acceptable. This term included the attempt to revive narrative and dramatic verse, in what was sometimes called the New Narrative.

Critical Overview

When "Supernatural Love" was first published in *The Lamplit Answer*, Rosetta Cohen, reviewing the book for *The Nation*, picked it out for appreciative comment: "Through the rigid symmetries of the tercets, Schnackenberg conflates the love of parent with the love of Christ, and the simplest actions—the child embroidering, the father searching out the Latin root of a word—become transcendent by way of the child's sudden, tiny self-inflicted wound." Since publication, the poem has often been reprinted in poetry anthologies and has been posted and discussed on various Internet poetry forums. When it was included in the selection of Schnackenberg's poems published under the title *Supernatural Love: Poems 1976–1992*, it attracted more favorable comment from reviewers. In *Poetry*, Christian Wiman declares it to be finest poem in the book and places it with some of Schnackenberg's other poems of the period as "a substantial and rare accomplishment. I think people will be reading some of these poems for a long time." Wiman adds, in a comment that could certainly apply to "Supernatural Love," " Schnackenberg's particular gift is for a kind of clear density, for making many different strands of experience part of a single, deceptively simple weave. Difficulty dissolves into the fluent lines and surprising rhymes of the finished poem."

In the *New York Review of Books*, Daniel

Mendelsohn has similar praise for "Supernatural Love" as "thematically ambitious … an intricately achieved meditation on poetry, time, love, and faith." Adam Kirsch, in the *New York Times Book Review*, also admires Schnackenberg for the ambitious nature of her poetry and comments in words that might well apply to "Supernatural Love": "Her verse is strong, dense and musical, anchored in the pentameter even when it veers into irregularity; behind it are formidable masters, Robert Lowell most notably, but also Yeats and Auden."

What Do I Read Next?

- Schnackenberg's first book, *Portraits and Elegies* (1982), marked her emergence as a poet who had mastered a wide variety of types of formal verse. Reviewers hailed this collection as evidence of an exciting new voice in American poetry. Many of the poems in this collection are more accessible for the general reader than some of Schnackenberg's complex later work.

- *Rebel Angels: 25 Poets of the New Formalism* (1996), edited by Mark Jarman and David Mason, is an anthology that brings together most of the major poets of the New Formalism. Curiously, the editors omit Schnackenberg. The poets represented include Tom Disch, Timothy Steele, Mary Jo Salter, Brad Leithauser, Marilyn Hacker, Molly Peacock, Sydney Lea, Dana Gioia, and Andrew Hudgins.
- In his introduction to *The Direction of Poetry: An Anthology of Rhymed and Metered Verse Written in the English Language since 1975* (1988), Robert Richman describes this collection as a celebration of a particular group of poets whose work is marked by their use of rhyme and meter. This is an important anthology that marked the rise of New Formalism in the 1980s. Seventy-six poets are represented, including Schnackenberg.
- *Poetry after Modernism* (1998), edited by Robert McDowell, is a

collection of fourteen essays by poet-critics who discuss contemporary poetry from a variety of points of view. The poets write for the general reader, without indulging in obscure critical jargon. Many of them are associated with New Formalism.

Sources

Cohen, Rosetta, Review of *The Lamplit Answer*, in the *Nation*, December 7, 1985, p. 621.

Dawson, Ariel, "The Yuppie Poet," in *Writer's Chronicle*, Vol. 14, No. 5, 1984.

Gioia, Dana, "Notes on the New Formalism," in *Expansive Poetry: Essays on the New Narrative & the New Formalism*, edited by Frederick Feirstein, Story Line Press, 1989, p. 164; originally published in the *Hudson Review*, Autumn 1987.

Kirsch, Adam, "All Eyes on the Snow Globe," in *New York Times Book Review*, October 29, 2000, p. 27.

McPhillips, Robert, "Reading the New Formalists," in *Sewanee Review*, Vol. 97, Winter 1989, p. 75.

————————, "What's New about the New Formalism?" in *Expansive Poetry: Essays on the New Narrative & the New Formalism*, edited by Frederick Feirstein, Story Line Press, 1989, pp. 195, 207; originally published in *Crosscurrents*, Vol. 8, No. 2, 1988.

Mendelsohn, Daniel, "Breaking Out," in the *New York Review of Books*, March 29, 2001, p. 39.

Schnackenberg, Gjertrud, "Supernatural Love," *The Lamplit Answer*, Farrar, Straus and Giroux, 1985, pp. 81-83.

Shetley, Vernon, *After the Death of Poetry: Poet*

and Audience in Contemporary America, Duke University Press, 1993, pp. 157, 190.

Turner, Frederick, and Ernst Pöppel, "The Neural Lyre: Poetic Meter, the Brain, and Time," in *Expansive Poetry: Essays on the New Narrative & the New Formalism*, edited by Frederick Feirstein, Story Line Press, 1989, pp. 240, 241, 249.

Viereck, Peter, "Strict Wildness: The Biology of Poetry," in *Poets & Writers Magazine*, Vol. 16, No. 3, May-June 1988, pp. 8, 11.

Wakoski, Diane, "The New Conservatism in American Poetry," in *American Book Review*, Vol. 8, No. 4, May-June 1986.

Wiman, Christian, Review of *Supernatural Love: Poems, 1976–1992*, in *Poetry*, Vol. 179, No. 2, November 2001, p. 91.

Further Reading

Finch, Annie, ed., *After New Formalism: Poets on Form, Narrative and Tradition*, Story Line Press, 1999.

This collection of twenty-four essays explores the formal possibilities of contemporary poetry and the implications of formalism for poetic history, practice, and theory. Contributors include Dana Gioia, Mark Jarman, David Mason, Marilyn Nelson, Molly Peacock, Adrienne Rich, and others.

Lake, Paul, "Return to Metaphor: From Deep Imagist to New Formalist," in *Southwest Review*, Vol. 74, Fall 1989, pp. 515-29.

Lake explores the different use of figurative language between the so-called deep image poets of the 1960s and 1970s and the New Formalists. He includes an analysis of Schnackenberg's poem "The Paperweight," from *Portraits and Elegies*.

McPhillips, Robert, *The New Formalism: A Critical Introduction*, Textos Books, 2005.

This study of New Formalist poetry and poetics includes chapters on

Schnackenberg ("Gjertrud Schnackenberg and the High Style"), Dana Gioia, Timothy Steele, and the verse satire of Tom Disch, R. S. Gwynn, and Charles Martin. There is also a comprehensive bibliography.

Schnackenberg, Gjertrud, "The Epistle of Paul the Apostle to the Colossians," in *Incarnation: Contemporary Writers on the New Testament*, edited by Alfred Corn, Penguin, 1990, pp. 189-211.

In this engaging, elegantly written essay, Schnackenberg discusses the historical and theological aspects of Paul's letter to the Colossians. The book as a whole includes similar essays by other writers and poets, including Dana Gioia, Amy Clampitt, John Updike, and Annie Dillard, in which they give their personal responses to other New Testament books.

Shapiro, Alan, "The New Formalism," in *Critical Inquiry*, Vol. 14, No. 1, Autumn 1987, pp. 200-13.

Shapiro argues that much of the poetry written by the New Formalists is metrically monotonous.

CPSIA information can be obtained
at www.ICGtesting.com
Printed in the USA
LVOW10s2002121117
556042LV00029B/259/P